T0113938

ECHOES FROM OUR HEAVENLY

HEAVENLY

God

MIKINSON HENRY

WESTBOW
PRESS®
A DIVISION OF THOMAS NELSON
& ZONDERVAN

WestBow Press books may be ordered through booksellers or by contacting:

WestBow Press
A Division of Thomas Nelson & Zondervan
1663 Liberty Drive
Bloomington, IN 47403
www.westbowpress.com
844-714-3454

ISBN: 978-1-6642-4579-2 (sc)
ISBN: 978-1-6642-4581-5 (hc)
ISBN: 978-1-6642-4580-8 (e)

Library of Congress Control Number: 2021919784

Print information available on the last page.

WestBow Press rev. date: 05/05/2022

Ecclesiastical Censor: The Reverend Leonardo J. Gajardo, JCL, STD

Ecclesiastical permission: The Most Reverend Robert John McClory, JD, JCL, DD

Bishop of Gary,
October 20, 2021

CONTENTS

ACKNOWLEDGMENTS

Reflective Readers: Bishop Robert J. McClory
                    Bishop Donald J. Hying (2019)
Bishop Emeritus Dale J. Melczek
Rev. Kevin M. Scalf, CPPS
Rev. Patrick J. Kalich
Rev. Kevin Huber, DMin
Rev. Tim Mcfarland, CPPS
Rev. Leonardo J. Gajardo, JCL, STD
                    Rev. Jeffrey Burton
                    Deacon Daniel Lowery, PhD
                    Deacon Martin J. Brown
                    Deacon Michael Cummings
                    Deacon Peter Znika, Jr.
                    Sr. Sallie Latkovich, SCJ
                    Sr. Joanne Marie Schutz, SSCM
                    Anthony M. Bonta, PhD
                    Barbara Lowery

Pelfrene Saint-Fort
Bastien Henry
Clara Henry
Lannie Cummings
Ingrid Znika
Merissaint Desliens
Mrs. Marian Weeks
Anicet Henry
Paul Rodney Henry
Joseph E. Ware
Mary S. Ware
Richard A. Hobby
Maudeline bolivar-Henry

Thomas James
Sandra Henry
Witny Henry
Lucien Mas Henry
Kerline Henry
Depeigne Henry
Disma Saint-Fort
Marie Yvrose Saint-Louis
Roseline Pierre Saint-Fort

Editor and proofreader: Megan Henry

PREFACE

This book is a continuation of *An Inspiration from God*. God has told me not to be afraid of obstacles that may come my way even when I am trying to spread his message. Struggles sometimes help you to become humbler in life. It can help you keep your focus on God. Never try to take the easy way out. Our Lord Jesus Christ suffered a great deal to bring the good news and the truth to his people. If Christ, who is the Son of God himself, has suffered such a great deal for doing good, you also may suffer. Always keep your head up; don't ever get discouraged in life. Stay positive, and always remember that God's light is closer to you than you think. God's love for us is never ending. If God never stops loving us, that should be sufficient for us to start loving him and each another, and to spread his love around the world. If we can embrace the love that God has for us, together we can say that God's desire for us to be with him for eternity will be fulfilled.

INTRODUCTION

*M*y hope is that these words will give you the ability and the capacity to see God in all the positive things you are involved in. May these words help bring you closer to God and his people around the world. May these words bring you wisdom, help you to be exemplary in our society today, and to have a positive impact on the lives of others. My hope is that this second edition will continue to inspire and strengthen you even more. I hope that this book will help you find your way to God or strengthen the connection that you already have with him and continue in the right direction.

I encourage you to help promulgate the message that is in this book to help others, to help raise their spirits and to help them to be a fully active player in God's plan. I hope that you will respond to the Lord's call by fulfilling your duties on earth and getting yourself and others prepared to meet your God when you leave this earth. God wants all of us to be with him in heaven, but we must direct our free will in a positive way for ourselves and for others in order to be in that beatific vision.

WHERE THERE IS LIGHT,
THERE IS GOD

Blue sky, moonlight, bright night: God is here.
Stars at night, light for the world to see your living presence.
Beautiful creatures on earth must be some of God's creations.

God's wind blows to bring fresh air and the great Spirit to his people.
Honesty and love are where his heart rests.
Purity and clarity are his nature.

Every note of his music can be heard around the world.
Every string of his orchestra is an exemplar to our society,
Ecliptically in tune with his love for his people.

There is always light where God is, and there is always love where
his radiance rests.

ETERNAL BLESSED

Eternal blessed, let your Spirit bless my soul and help me reach a new phase.
Reign in my world, and bring to life a soul that was lost and into a world that has just begun.
Eternal blessed, pity is your mercy, love is your kindness, and Spirit is your light that gives clarity.

Eternal blessed, grace is your continuity of greatness and love for your children.
Reign in my great matters, and let your Spirit bring me to life when I am not there.
Eternal blessed, live in my heart and rest in my soul forever blessed.

WHEN YOU KNOW YOU
HAVE FRIENDS

When your friends are in distress, show them love.
When your friends are in sorrow, commiserate with them.
When your friends are in quagmires, help them get out.

When your friends are confused, be the first one to shed the light on them.
When your friends are in trouble, be the first one to come to their rescue.
When your friends are lost, be the first one to help bring them back to themselves.

When your friends are in darkness, be the first one to help them see the light with the help of God.
When your friends are drowning, be the first one to help them swim out of it.
When your friends have no wings to fly, be the first one to help them see God.

DIVINE LOVE AND SPIRIT

Love divine, come be our rest.
Spirit wise, bring us new lives.
Love divine, live in our hearts.
Spirit wise, come bless us now.

Love divine, bring us new hopes.
Spirit wise, make our minds fresh.
Love divine, cure us all now.
Spirit wise, rest in our minds.

Love divine, make us brand new.
Spirit wise, save our lost souls.

YOURS

Your angels are blessed, and heaven is their nest.
Your Spirit is rested in those who are blessed.
Your place is the nest where your birds live and rest.

Your grace is the blessing that feeds all your birds.
Your children are blessed when heaven is their bread.
Your covenant is rested in your sanctuary nest.

FOUNTAIN OF LOVE AND PEACE

Fountain of love, flow in our hearts, and bring us to new life.
Fountain of peace, flow in our minds, and help bring tranquility to our lives.
Fountain of love, bring us new hope when we are in despair.

Fountain of love, help us to complete your tasks, and help your children to see your grace.
Fountain of peace, rescind all the things that are not in cohesiveness with your law and your kingdom.
Fountain of love, feed us the bread that will bring us to eternal life.

Fountain of love, make us walk on water like you.
Fountain of peace, let your children see the wonders of your works and your goodness.
Fountain of love, let your wings be the umbrella of our safety.

KING OF THE UNIVERSE

Christ is here!
Christ is born, heaven-brought joy.
Christ on the cross suffered for love.[1]
Christ's death arrived, bringing new life.
"Christ is risen,"[2] believers have hoped.
"Christ is ascended to heaven,"[3] and joy has arrived.
"Christ is in heaven";[4] heaven's gate is opened for all his faithful.
Christ is love; his love shows it all.
"Christ is the Alpha and the Omega!"[5] You
can be part of his company, too,
if you follow his law.
Christ is the testimony of the life that God
had given to us, so that we too
have a chance to meet his Father.
Christ is ever present; his love exemplifies that by his actions.
"Christ is near,"[6] so better prepare yourselves for his coming.
"Christ is our Savior";[7] in him salvation is within reach.
Christ is the gift that the Blessed Mother
accepted for us out of love.
Christ is the king that "the world cannot contain."[8]
Christ is the light that leads us to his Father.
Christ is the fresh and pure water that
flows through us from heaven.
Christ is the one that we should be searching
for to give us what we need.
Christ is the life of the Spirit that can be in each heart.
Christ is what makes peace reign in the
world to revitalize our spirits.

1 First Jn 3:16 NABRE.
2 Mt 28:7 NJB.
3 Acts 1:9–11 NJB.
4 Acts 1:11 NJB.
5 Rv 22:13 NJB.
6 Lk 21:31 NJB.
7 Lk 2:11 NABRE.
8 First Kgs 8:27 NJB.

HEAVEN IS OPEN

Heaven is open for all the faithful to see.
Heaven is open for those who know the Father, the Son, and the Holy Spirit.
Heaven is open for those who follow his law and precepts.
Heaven is open for all his children to "come to the feast."[9]

Heaven is open for those who abide by his law.
Heaven is open for all those who have the divine spirit of the Trinity.
Heaven is open for all who are on the right track to be sanctified.

Heaven is open for our hopes and dreams to come alive.
Heaven is open to welcome us with everlasting joy.
Heaven is open for all to come to the beatific vision.
Heaven is open for all the clean and pure ones to stay in his sanctuary as his company.

---

[9] Mt 22:2, 4 NJB.

YOU CAN MAKE ME LIKE YOU

Jesus, you turned water into wine;[10] you can transform my spirit into goodness.

You made the blind man see;[11] you can make me see light in the darkness.

You transformed two fish and three loaves of bread sufficient to feed more than five thousand people[12] when there was a paucity of food to feed them.

You can help me to be strong enough and give me all that I need to feed your sheep and your lambs.[13]

You astonished the doctors at the temple at the age of twelve[14] and showed them your great knowledge of the word of God.

Help me to grasp your Word in a clearer way in order to better present it to your people.

You have brought so many things to life, you can transform me to be like you.

You raised Lazarus from the dead;[15] you can raise my mind, body, and soul[16] to a new life.

---

[10] Jn 2:1–11 NABRE.
[11] Mk 8:23 NABRE.
[12] Mt 14:17–21 NJB.
[13] Jn 21:15–17 NJB
[14] Lk 2:46–47 NJB.
[15] Jn 11:38–44 NABRE.
[16] Lk 10:27 NJB.

YOU THINK YOU KNOW GOD?

You think you know God? Embrace his love, his company, and his children too.
You think you know God? Welcome his people with arms open.
You think you know God? Serve him to the fullness; love his gospel and his Church.

You think you know God? Open your heart to his teaching, and conform yourself to his law.
You think you know God? Stop fooling yourself because you cannot fool God.
When "the ladder day"[17] comes, you will have a clear path between heaven and hell.
You think you know God? Stop pretending, and follow his lead.

You think you know God? Do everything according to his book.
You think you know God? Forget and forgive when others are at fault.
You think you know God? Be the exemplary for others to "see the goodness of God in you."[18]

---

[17] Gn 28:12 NABRE.
[18] Ps 27:13 NABRE.

CONTRIBUTION

Have you ever thought about your contribution to the beauty of God's kingdom?
Have you ever thought about all the good things that you can bring to the table?
Have you ever thought about being a paragon and having a positive influence on many?

Have you ever felt that "fire burning inside your heart"[19] to carry out the Lord's message across the globe?
Have you ever thought about carrying "the Image of God"[20] in "your heart, mind, body, and soul"?[21]
Have you ever seen the grace of God pouring on his people?

Have you ever thought about how much love the Holy Father has for you?
Why are you waiting to be a participant at the feast? Don't be a bystander! Great talents are not to be wasted, and nor are great minds! It's time to step up to the plate and be that child of God because he wants you to help change the world.

---

[19] Jer 20:9 NABRE.
[20] Ws 1:23 NJBRE.
[21] Lk 10:27 NJB.

WHAT CAN YOU DO FOR GOD AND HIS PEOPLE?

What can you do for God, for humanity, yourself, and his people?
Can you help bring peace to the world and help others live in God's Spirit?
Can you help lead God's people in a more acute way to help facilitate his works?

Can you excel in God's missions throughout the world?
Can you have the passion that is in God's framework and his vision?
Can you let his love manifest in you and let your heart be surrendered to his plans?

Can you see the world in the circumference of God's vision?
Can you help the love of God flow abundantly to those areas that are lacking?
Can you give that unlimited effort to God's work on earth and never get lethargic when performing your duties?

ETERNAL AND TRIUMPHANT GOD

Triumphant God, conquer a world that is in shambles and desperately needs your guidance.

Eternal God, conquer our hearts, and bring new life into our world that is so lacking judgments.

Triumphant God, make straight our path for the coming of our Lord, Jesus Christ.

Eternal God, emancipate "our mind, body and soul"[22] from our obtuse ways of thinking.

Triumphant God, help us to see the big picture that is right in front of us.

Eternal God, make us, "your rock like Peter,"[23] and help us to see the light in order to welcome others to your kingdom.

Triumphant God, bring your infinite love inside our "hearts, minds, and souls."

Eternal God, give us the ability to see your grace and goodness in all of your creatures.

Triumphant God, let us be part of your light, and make us your saints forever.

---

[22] Lk 10:27 NJB.
[23] Mt 16:18 NABRE.

BETTER GET TO KNOW GOD

The wind does not blow in a clustered space: It is the same way love does not cherish in you if you keep it to yourself.

Do you have anything good in you when you are preaching violence and feeding venom to God's children to hurt one another?

You cannot see the fullness of God's love if you do not meet him part of the way.

It's the same way that a stream cannot flow at its normal pace if there are obstacles in its path.

You cannot see God eye to eye if you do not love His people.

You cannot help your fellow citizens if you don't have the willingness to do so.

You cannot live forever if you cannot join his assembly.

It's the same way that you cannot see the full mystery of God if you are not one of his Holy ones.

You cannot know God if you do not know his people!

LEAD ME TO YOU, LORD

"Lord, lead me,"[24] I am a "lost sheep."[25]
I do not know where to begin and where to finish.
I do know where I am from, but I do not know where I am going.
I do not know how to love like you; help me, "make me one of your own."[26]

I do not know how to spread your love. Let your abundant love into my heart, let your love reign on my spirit, let your sun brighten my day, and let your light be the way and guidance for all that I am.
Let your Spirit embrace me and be my light in the midst of darkness.
Let your food be my bread on a continual basis.
Let your grace pour out on me so that I can see your goodness.

Let me live and die in your loving arms.
Let your wings be my umbrella of love, spirit, and safety.
Let your optical views be my eyes and vision in times of obscurity.
Let my, "mind, body, and soul,"[27] abide in your Spirit always and never distance myself from you.

---

[24] Ps 5:8–9 NIV.
[25] Lk 15:4–6 NABRE.
[26] Is 64:7 NJB.
[27] Lk 10:27 NJB.

YOU ARE NOT CLOSE TO GOD
WHEN FEEDING THE BEAST

When your world is contrary to God's Spirit and love, you are not close to God.

When everything you do is creating propaganda and hate, you are not close to God.

When prejudice is your everyday nutrient, you are not close to God.

When you can't even shake hands with your brothers and sisters in church, you are not close to God.

When there is not love but hate inside of you, you are not close to God.

When you cannot welcome the children of God, you are not close to God.

When your insanity and imbecility take over your common sense, you are not close to God.

When human lives and animals do not have any meaning to you, you are not close to God.

When your world is not at peace, you look for trouble wherever you go, you are not close to God.

When you presume, make fallacious assumptions and dubious claims, you are not close to God.

When God's Spirit is not in you, you are not close to God.

GOD'S WIND

"God's wind blows"[28] where He wants it to bring fresh air to his people. You cannot change the course of God's wind or change his outpouring love.

You cannot change the course of God or change the course of what God wants for his children.

You cannot change the grace that God pours on his children.

How long will it take for you to realize that your way is not God's way? You cannot change the world in to your madness.

You cannot continue to be an advocate for Satan; otherwise, there will be nothing but hell for you.

Now is the time to change your course and follow God. God is the only one who can save you.

Can't you see that you cannot hamper the love that God wants for each of his children to cherish?

You cannot change God because he is your Maker, your Supreme Leader, he is immutable and unchangeable, but you can change your actions for good.

You can change your way of thinking and start to embrace God by trying not to shut the door on others.

You can only be a true servant of God if you obey his law and his precepts.

You can only be a true servant of God if you start treating his people equally.

You can only be a true servant of God when you don't have special preferences.

You can truly serve God when you can fully understand and see what God stands for.

What would it take for you to see the light?

---

[28] Jn 3:8 NJB.

THE WORLD HAS ITS PACE

Can't you see that the world is changing at the speed of light?
You need to change for the better in your community and your society.
Can't you see that we approach things differently now?
You can't stay in your archaic way of thinking.

You ought to change for good, for the love of God, yourself, and others.
You want to see positive results and move forward; you ought to change your way of living.
You can only move forward if you allow the Spirit of God to metamorphose your life and be your ultimate vehicle for success and endurance.
Don't look for ostensible reasons to carry the hate inside your heart; look for God! He is the answer. If you allow God, he will guide you and lead you to the right path.

DON'T BE THE ONE WITHOUT A PLAN

Don't be so pliant to their agendas, propaganda, demagoguery, and their false teachings.

Don't be so gullible to everything that comes out of their mouths. Listen to God, and He will lead you in the right direction.

Don't be so obstinate to hear "the Good News."[29] Listen to God, and He will teach you

Don't live like a man with no plan, no future, and have nothing to live for. Use your talent to the fullest and search for God. He will show you the Way.

Don't be like a man with no acuteness, no logic, and no philosophical thinking. Look for God, and He will bright your day.

Don't get stuck in the game with the devil. Search for God, and He will spare you and guide your path.

Let God's Spirit take over your life and your future. Your life will be whiter than a snowflake.

---

[29] 1 Cor 15:1 NABRE.

DON'T GET DUPED BY THE DEVIL

Don't get subsumed into the devil's game. Don't let the devil parachute your soul into his own agenda. Come to God: God is waiting to show you love.

Even when you are at odds with God, God is waiting for you with his arms open to welcome you back.

Don't be too gullible to dubious impressions and teachings that have been engineered by the devil. God is waiting to save your soul.

Don't fall for that traps that the devil has stored for you. God is waiting to bring your life back to earth again.

Even when you engage in sophistry, mudslinging, and fallacious pretext, God is waiting to embrace you.

Don't get saturated in the paltriness of the devil. God is waiting to make you brand new.

Don't get involved in the chicaneries of the devil. God is waiting to lead you to the right path.

Even when you are in a quandary and can't seem to find your rhythm, God is waiting to show you how it's done.

Now is the propitious time to "surrender yourself to God so that you can be saved,"[30] and get yourself prepared for eternal life.

---

[30] Rom 6:13 NABRE.

THE KINGDOM OF GOD

The kingdom of God is where love is cherished.
The kingdom of God is where great minds think alike.
The kingdom of God is where prejudice, crime, and hate are obsolete.

The kingdom of God is where love never ends.
The kingdom of God is where his people are blessed.
The kingdom of God is where there is purity, sincerity, and infinity.

The kingdom of God is where love is at work!

LORD, CAN YOU SHOW ME THE WAY?

Can you show me how to care for your people and to carry your love inside of me?
Can you show me how to be adept at the mission that you have for me?

Can you show me how to be pragmatic in everything that I undertake?
Can you show me how to deal with arduous tasks, complex problems with ease and calm?
Can you show me how to make good conjectures even when I don't have a clue?

Can you show me your kingdom when I leave this earth?
Can your Father be proud of the work that I have done on earth? Will I see him face-to-face?
Will the feast begin when you are welcoming me at your golden palace?

Can I see the fullness of your love when the day comes and live with you for eternity?

DON'T IMITATE THE DEVIL

The world is so wry; so is the devil.
Myopic thinking is so lame; so is the devil.
A malicious mind cannot differentiate right and wrong; nor can the devil.

You have your own circle of hate groups; so does the devil.
You can't seem to do anything right; so does the devil.
There is only evil in your eyes; so has the devil.

Don't think like the devil; think like God.
Get closer to God because you need God in your life, and He is the only one who can save you.

OUT OF WHACK

Why are you so irascible at the world? Is the Spirit of God not in you? Why are you so flippant to everyone of God's creations that come in your proximity?

Why are you so angry at the world when you have contributed to the destruction that is taking place in the world?

Why are you so cantankerous and can't see the big picture? Why can't you see that "you need to be born again, in God's Spirit"?[31] Why can't you see that your world is in chaos and needs to be rescued?

Do you want your world to be at peace, your heart to beat at a normal pace, and your lungs to breathe normally? Start seeing God in everything good that is around you!

Start carrying yourself in the manner that is supposed to be and come closer to God and, "He will instruct you and show you the way you should walk"![32]

---

[31] Jn 3:3–5 NIV.
[32] Ps 32:8 NABRE.

CANTICLE OF MIKINSON

My spirit rests in the Lord for he never lets me down.
When trouble is at my doorstep, I have a safe place to hide.

He spreads his wings to efface the clouds of darkness and to protect
his children.
He lets the evil cloud and the evildoers know who is in command.

He turns all evildoers and those with malicious intents into dust with
his power and might.
He keeps his children at his side all day long.

What a marvelous God who never abandons his children,
Even when missteps may be their everyday routine.

All who follow him will be blessed with his grace and infinite love.
His presence and abundance of love will live for eternity.

WHY NOT CHANGE FOR THE BETTER?

Why are you are so languor; the Word of God is not in your soul?
Why are you so apathetic; the Word of God is not in your spirit?
Why are you so lethargic; the Spirit of God is not in you?

Why are you so close-minded with your astigmatic views and actions;
the Spirit of God is not at your tent?
If you are not so acute with your evil mind, come to the Father; he
will make you bright like a star.
You can only improve and stay above the water when you are closer
to God and his Spirit.

WHY BE SO NEGATIVE? STAY POSITIVE

Why are you so officious and always disregard the effort of others?
Why are you so egotistical that you can't seem to acknowledge the talents of others?
Why do you think that everyone is backward and awkward, except you?

Why are you so pessimistic about everything that is not in your interest?
Why is your mind so troubled when you can be at peace and cohesive with the Spirit of God?
Why can't you see that your behavior is not God's way?

Why can't you conform yourself in, "the image and likeness of God"?[33]
Why can't you get your act together for the love of God and others?
Why can't you see that you are also part of God's plan and missions?

Why can't you allow your God, your Lord's Spirit, to dwell in your, "mind, body, and soul"?[34]

[33] Ws 1:23 NJB.
[34] Lk 10:27 NJB.

IT CAN ONLY BE POSSIBLE
WITH YOUR HELP

O God, my heart can only beat when I am, "under the shadow of your wings."[35]
My lungs can only breathe when you are in my life.
O Lord, my eyes can only see when your visions are in me.

O God, my mind can only think when your Spirit is in me.
My heart can only love when you help me and show me how to love.
O Lord, I can only function when you are around and escape the darkness when you show me the light.

O God, I can only be saved when you embrace me, love me, take me in your arms, and let me be that child.
My spirit can only be true when I can be your servant, your student, the facilitator of your plans.
O Lord, let me be, "the apple of your eye,"[36] and let your radiance love brighten my day.

---

[35] Ps 17:8 NABRE.
[36] Ps 17:8 NABRE.

STOP DOING THE DEVIL'S WORK

You do not know much about a man of God.
You do not know much about a man that God chose to be his servant.
You are fooling yourself if you think that you can stop God's will and destiny for his children.

You do not know much about being a true servant of God.
Why is it not clicking in your great matters? You must be working for the devil.
Just remember that God's train goes faster than a bullet train and much faster than the speed of light.

You can't close the door that God has opened for his children.
You can't stop the will of God. If you are trying to do so, something has to give, and it will be you in your end.
You can only be saved if you stay in God's Spirit and presence.

WHATEVER YOU DO IS GOOD WHEN IT'S CLOSER TO GOD'S MESSAGE

Repetition is not a bad thing if it can bring the message across.
Competition can be good, but only when it falls under the banner of unity, in the Trinity.
Admiration can also be a great thing, but only when it's in the Spirit of God.

Explanation can also shed the light on the blind, but only when it's factual.
Exaltation can surely be the transformation of God's grace through you, which can only mean one thing—that God's message is purely and unequivocally heard.

THE ONE WITHOUT GRAVITY
WILL NOT STAND

You have no ground when you are out of the circumference of God's message.

You are like an empty sack that tries to stand on a flat surface and would have even a greater risk of falling on a slippery slope.

You can only stand when the Spirit of God is in you and your willingness, and when you dedicate your efforts to his missions.

If you don't have a good foundation or base, you have nothing to begin with. The strength of that gravity unifies its base and makes it firm. If you don't have that balance and gravity to make you stand on your own, you will not be standing.

It is the same way when you are willing to unify your soul with God's Spirit. There is not one ground that you can't stand on, there is not one mountain that you can't climb, and there is not one obstacle that you can't overcome.

The message for you is to stay in God's presence and Spirit, and you will see the grace of God.

ARE YOU DOING THE GOOD WORK?

Are you spreading God's love around the globe and helping spread His words?

Are you getting God's message to his people to help them see what is right?

Can you be one of God's sagacious disciples who bring nothing but the good news to God's people?

Are you one of God's servants, "who came to serve and not to be served," just like our Savior, Jesus "The Christ"?[37]

Are you "proclaiming the gospel enough and doing good to all who are in dire need"?[38] If you are, your journey to "the kingdom of God" has just begun.

Can you clearly see and understand the plan and the mission of God that you are undertaking?

---

[37] Mk 10:45 NJB.
[38] Gal 6:10 NABRE.

HEAVEN IS NEAR

Heaven is near when my mother will bring me the good news.
Heaven is near when I get to hear God's message before I leave my flesh on earth.
Heaven is near when I get a glimpse the Father, the Son, and the Holy Spirit.

Heaven is near when there is nothing but purity, honesty, and sincerity in your sanctuary.
Heaven is near when God's blessings will be fully poured into my soul.
Heaven is near when his orchestra will play one of its finest pieces to welcome me.

Heaven is near when there is nothing but an ebullient look on my face.
Heaven is near when I see nothing but your grace and love around me.
Heaven is near when I fully become one of your saints.

RESPECT HIS HOUSE

You see all these great things around?
Don't you know that this is holy ground?
Why are you trying to desecrate this beautiful place of your Holy Father?

Don't you know that this is the house of God? Why can't you give him full respect and carry his words in your heart?
Don't you know that "his words can set you free"[39] for eternity if you follow them closely?
Don't you know that his words changed many hearts and brought purity and love where there was none?

Why are you trying to alter his message around the world?
Don't you know that there is no dichotomy between his law and his love?
Don't you know that "there no other God like Him" and, "his kingdom will stand forever"?[40]

Respect God, his message, and his law, and you might have the chance to meet him one day.

---

[39] Jn 8:32 NJB.
[40] Dn 2:44 NABRE.

CHANGE YOUR EARTHLY WAY OF DOING THINGS, AND COME TO GOD

You are in an earthly world!

If you have no ground, then your mind is empty.

If your mind has no ground to stand on, then your speech is incapable of bringing the good news to God's people.

If your speech does not make a positive impact and influence, then that fire is being extinguished inside your heart.

If you don't have the Spirit of God in you, then you are like an egg, rolling on sharp blades because you are already in the land of the dead.

What will it take for you to realize that your way is not God's way?

Your obsession to worldly things is not God's way.

What will it take for you to see God eye to eye and be with him for all eternity?

What will it take for you to come to the feast?

What will it take for you to give up all the vanities and win your soul?

What will it take for you conform in the Spirit of God?

You can astonish everyone with the presence of God in your soul and help others to see God's goodness in your heart.

WISDOM

What is wisdom?

Could it be something ecliptic, mystic, and Christocentric that is originated from the Trinity?

Could it be something apodictic, unequivocally clean, and pure?

Could it be that energetic fire in our heart that is ready to do good and spread God's love to his people?

Could it be the knowledge, the patience, and the other virtues that spread out from God's love?

Could it be one of the gifts from God that helps us to carry out his message?

Could it be the grace and the love that God pours out on all his children?

ETERNAL GOD, MAKER OF ALL

Eternal God, help us to love.
Maker of all, open our hearts.
Eternal God, purify our souls.

Eternal God, your blessings bring us joy.
Maker of all, let your children see your rainbows of love.
Eternal God, levitate our thoughts and renew our faith.

Eternal God, life is originated from you.
Maker of all, your peace is your love.
Eternal God, save our world now because it is lost.

WHY DO YOU CALL GOD ONLY
WHEN YOU ARE IN NEED?

You called God when your house caught on fire and ignored God when He provided you what you needed.
You called God when you were in a quandary and ignored God when your problems were solved.
You called God when your world was upside down and ignored God after He rescued you.

You called God when your river ran dry and ignored God when He quenched your thirst.
You called God when your heart was in trouble and ignored God after He brought tranquility to your tent.
Why don't you call your God at all times and not just when you are in trouble?

Let God be the air that you breathe, the sound that beats in your heart, and the mind that makes the right decision at all times.

CAN YOU DO WHAT IS RIGHT?

Can "peace flow"[41] into your soul to bring new understanding and new life in you?
Can love be at the center of your actions to make your Father proud?
Can peace be manifested in you to make your God proud?

Can love help us all to bolster our strengths and our admiration for God?
Can you not be deceived by the devil and be an astute servant of God?
Can you not let Satan be your mountebank and turn yourself to God?

Can you not be a perfunctory worker and, "serve God with all you heart, mind, and soul"?[42]
Can you not be so mundane? Can you stay with God and only God?
Can you turn over your soul to God that can save you?

Can you see the light that is in reach?

---

41 Is 66:12 NJB.
42 Lk 10:27 NJB.

FOR THE LOVE OF GOD

For the love of God, "The Father," yourself, and others, change your way of living.
For the love of the Son, treat your fellow citizens with dignity and respect.
For the love of the Holy Spirit, be a role model for God's children.

For the love of humanity, live in peace and harmony with your brothers and sisters.
For the love of God, restore the trust that your beloved friends and your fellow citizens have in you.
For the love God, let God's angels help you fly on earth.

For the love of God, let your name be known for great philanthropic works on earth and let the Spirit of God be your guidance.
For the love of God, let God be the vehicle that will lead you to the right path.

THANK YOU, FATHER

Thank you, God, for being the Father that you are to me.
You gave me hope when I was in despair.
You kept your eyes on me at all times, while I was invisible to others.
You showed me love when others gave me grief.
You opened your doors for me, while others were closing theirs.

You offered me encouragement, while others gave me discouragement.
You brought me up, while others tried to bring me down.
You gave me wings, while others tried to shoot me down.
You made me fly, while others tried to keep me in a fledgling state.
You gave me love, when others wanted no part of me.

I am always blessed when you are around.

HOW CAN I?

How can I return the love to you, Father?

I can return the love when I follow your law and precepts.
I can return the love when I stay away from sin.
I can return the love when I treat my brothers and sisters with dignity and respect.

I can return the love when your mission becomes my mission.
I can return the love when I follow your directions and obey your law.
I can return the love when I become part of you, and my life will rise up to another level.

I can return the love when I, "do the things that are acceptable to you and pleasing to your eyes."[43]

---

[43] Eph 5:10 NABRE.

IF I CAN DO THE NECESSARY THINGS

If I follow your footprints, I can be diligent.

If I persevere, I can be adept at anything that needs attention.

If I follow your vision and your Spirit, I can be very pragmatic in the analytical world.

If I can take one elephantine step closer, I can reach my destination.

If I am in the right mind and spirit, I can make better decisions and will be able to serve your people better.

If I continue to use the word "if," I will never get anywhere. It's time to make my voice heard and my actions count.

It's time to follow the One who had created me out of love.

It's time to start working for, "the kingdom of God,"[44] and give it all to almighty God for my own future.

---

[44] Dn 7:27 NABRE.

VISION

Vision of a man who never waivers.
Vision of a man who serves God with all his heart.
Vision of a man who sees God eye to eye.

Vision of a man whose God's works are priorities in his life.
Vision of a man who carries out God's missions.
Vision of a man who loves the Lord with all his heart.

Vision of a man who sees his future in heaven.

GOD'S LOVE

God's love spreads among his children to gives them life.
God's love lives among his children to make them breathe.
God's love reigns among his children.

God's love brings joy in a house full of troubles.
God's love is what the world needs to share and to change the status quo.
God's love saves many lives on earth.

God's love is, "the living water,"[45] the life among us.

---

[45] Jn 4:10–11 NJB.

STAY ALERT

Stay alert when the devil is in action!

Stay alert when the devil is spreading hate around!
Stay alert when the fraudulent one tries to manipulate others to be the devil's advocate.
Stay alert when the devil is at your doorstep.

Stay alert when the devil is spreading lies to trick your mind and others.

Stay alert and vigilant against all obstacles that the devil tries to lay on your path.
Stay alert when the devil tries to infuse your mind with all sorts of negativity.
Stay alert when the devil tries to infiltrate your soul into his madness.

Stay focused when God chooses you to be his servant and to protect his children on earth.

A TRUE SERVANT OF GOD

You embrace me with God's love when others see me as a stranger.
You welcome me at God's table when I am sometimes on the outside looking in and wondering if I am just dreaming.
You give me positive advice and help me see God's light when I get discouraged and don't feel like I am even welcome.
You symbolize God's Spirit, like, "the Great teacher of the law Gamaliel at Sanhedrin,"[46] who spoke the truth and brought good news to God's people according to God's law.

You show me the true face of God and Spirit while others are playing politics.
You have the mindset of a bishop in a deacon's stole.
Your pot in heaven is metamorphosizing while doing God's work and philanthropic missions on earth.
You make heaven smile when you spread God's love to his people.
When it's time for you to leave this earth, heaven will smile for a third time (your birth, your service to the world, and your welcoming to heaven). God will welcome you with open arms, and his symphony orchestra will play a masterpiece to welcome you in his sanctuary.

---

[46] Acts 5:34–41 NABRE.

TAKE A GOOD LOOK

Take a good look at the stars in the sky, and tell me there is not a living God.

Take a look at the sun that is brightening the day in every country and continent, and tell me there is not a God.

Take a look at the ocean, the earth, the sweet waters, and the lakes, and tell me that God does not exist.

Take a look at the animated principle of plant lives, and tell me that God is not around.

Take a look at the animals on earth, and tell me that there is not a God.

Take a look at all the great minds and all the science that God allows us to decode, and tell me that God is nowhere near us.

Take a look at yourself and other human beings, who are God's greatest creations on earth, and tell me that God does not exist.

Are you hallucinating, or you just not getting the truth?

Now is the time for you to come to grip that your Father exists. Now is the time for you to be saved; now is the time for you to come to know your Father. Now is the time for you not to leave yourself behind. Now it's the time for you make the right decision and to embrace God with all your heart.

LOOKING AT YOUR ACTIONS

Looking at your eyes try to find God's love.
Looking at your face to see if God's Spirit is in you.
Looking at you actions to see if you are a man of God.

Looking at your thoughts to see if great minds think alike.
Looking at your vision to see if it came from God.
Looking at your soul to see if you really follow God.

Looking at your world to see if God is in you.

HELP YOUR SOUL

Levitate your obtuse thinking with God's Spirit.
Alleviate your closed-mindedness with kindness and God's love.
Levitate your soul that is in desperate need of God's intervention.

Levitate your ambivalent thinking, and do good at all times.
Alleviate your thinking about seeing, "the kingdom of God."[47]
Levitate your illogical mind with common sense and God's love.

Levitate your whole world with God's love and Spirit.

---

[47] Dn 7:27 NABRE.

HIS SPIRIT AND VISION

When the Spirit of God is in you, his love is in you too.
When God's vision is in you, your mind thinks like God's children.
When the Spirit of God is in you, you see things with a different perspective.

When the Spirit of God is in you, you will begin to flourish in a more beautiful and prolific way.
When God's vision is in you, nebulous ideas are not your mission.
When the Spirit of God is in you, you are in a different place and stage.

When the Spirit of God and his vision are in you, people begin to see God's face in you, and you'll begin to love like God.

YOUR EGO?

Your egotistical mind can hamper your progress toward goodness. Your saturnine world can close and rescind your opportunity to do good for the love of God.

Your egotistical mind can bring darkness where there is light.

Your egotistical mind can close some doors that you don't even know are open.

Your saturnine world can confuse and bring anger to the world.

Your egotistical mind can plunge your good intentions to dilapidation.

Stay away from this kind of malignance; focus on God like a laser instead. See God and his people before seeing yourself; if you can do that, then you are on the right track.

LIFE BEFORE DEATH

Before death there is life.
You can bring a smile before people lose faith.
Before death there is life.
You still have a chance to be resurrected and stay in God's presence.

Before death there is life.
You can help save those who are about to perish because of the route that they chose.
Before death there is life.
Every sinner has a, "path to salvation,"[48] if they truly repent and don't blow it away.

Before death there is life.
There is a chance to rescind all the madness in you before making wrong decisions.
Before death there is life.
You can help build that great relationship with God and stay away from bad intentions.

---

[48] Rom 1:16 NABRE.

LIFE AFTER DEATH

After death there is life
Only if you follow the right path that will lead you to God.

After death life exists
Only if you don't do anything that will separate you from God forever.

After death life begins.
Only if you do what is acceptable to God, and you truly repent of all
your sins, then you will have the opportunity to live with your Father
forever.

After death life may flourish
Only if you know what your Father has in store for you in that beatific
vision.

After death life can be joyful
Only if you are one of the chosen ones, who does everything according
to God's law and precepts.

WHEN THE LORD COMES

When the Lord comes, your faith will be your passport to heaven.

When the Lord comes, all of God's adversaries will perish forever.
When the Lord comes, there will be no more pain for his children and his believers.
When the Lord comes, those who love him will see the reality in heaven.

When the Lord comes, there will be ramifications for those who did not follow his law.

When the Lord comes, the fire will be so hot and so high that it will be like lava from an erupting volcano.
When the Lord comes, he will be visible to all his children.
When the Lord comes, you cannot put a foot on that ladder if you are not one of his own.

When the Lord comes, all of his chosen ones will be saints in heaven.
When the Lord comes, there will be an infinite place for his children to live eternally.
When the Lord comes, violations of his law will be obsolete.

When the Lord comes, heaven will smile with great joy while welcoming God's children.

STAY AWAY FROM ALL THE
EARTHLY THINGS

You are so dependent on everything around you; that is not a good way to function.

You cannot spend a day without electronics: Do you think that is the way to live your life?

You cannot spend a day without complaining: Do you think that is God's way?

You cannot spend a day without the obsession of vanity: Do you think that is what God wants for you?

You cannot spend a day without talking about that superfluous paper: Do you think that life depends only on money?

You cannot spend one day without talking about some who are monetarily and earthly rich but spiritually poor: Do you think that God cherishes that?

You are doing all these things that are unnecessary and will lead you to nowhere.

Can you spend a day with God and continue to do so in the near future?

LIVING IN A FANTASY WORLD

Living in a fantasy world, when you think that your feet cannot touch the ground.
Living in a fantasy world, when you think that you are better than everyone else.
Living in a fantasy world, when you think you are above everyone else.

Living in a fantasy world, when you are the advocate of the devil.
Living in a fantasy world, when you carry on the devil's work throughout your life on earth.
Living in a fantasy world, when you think that everything in you is perfect, and no one else exists but you.

Living in a fantasy world, when you are having dinner with the devil and disregard God's law and precepts.
Living in a fantasy world, when you think you can rocket your way into heaven.
It is time for you to analyze your nebulous ideas and this fantasy world that you are living.
Come to God! God is waiting for you to save your poor soul.

WHEN WILL YOU KNOW?

When will you know that "the kingdom of God's is at hand,"[49] and you need to do something to protect your own soul?

When will you know that you need to grow good seed so that you can harvest a great crop?

When will you know you that the time is now to see the reality and have better understanding of God's kingdom?

When will you know that your effort can help save many live and empty souls?

When will you know that your effort can help feed many who are hungry for God's message?

When will know that you can be a part God's mission and make your dream come true?

When will you know that God needs you to strengthen his kingdom?

---

[49] Mk 1:15; Mt 3:2 NABRE.

PRINCE OF HOPE, LOVE, AND PEACE

"Prince of peace,"[50] hear us all our questions.
Prince of hope, spare all our lives.
Price of love, plea for our cases.

"Prince of peace," give us a spirit of love.
Prince of hope, make our paths straight.
Prince of love, live in our lives.

Prince of hope, love and peace bless us all now.

---

[50] Is 9:5 NABRE.

HEAVENLY KING

Heavenly King, come to my life.
Heavenly hope, quell our despair.
Heavenly King, let your love meet our willingness.

Heavenly King, let you children taste your goodness and your love.
Heavenly hope, give your children wings to fly.
Heaven King, give us the power to overcome evil.

Heavenly King, let us adore your presence and your Spirit.

WHY NOT STAY IN GOD'S SPIRIT?

Why imitate the devil when you can imitate God?
Why let the devil take over your life when you can be with God?
Why show off your sacred body to the whole world when you can show it to the one that you love?
Why destroy each other's lives when you did not create life?

Why follow the devil when you can be in God's hands?
Why stay in the dark when you can come to the light?
Why is hate your agenda when the love of God can be assimilated in your soul?
Why destroy your soul when you can pave the way and prepare yourself to live with your Father in heaven for eternity?

EVERYTHING GOOD THAT IS YOURS, BELONGS TO GOD

Your blessing is God's blessing, unless you refuse to be blessed and receive the grace of God.

Your journey is God's happiness unless you are making your journey in the path of the furnace.
Your vision is God's vision unless you stop seeing great things.
Your mission is God's mission unless you are giving up trying.

Your effort is God's effort unless you put it to rest.
Your love is God's love unless you stop, "loving God' your neighbors and yourself."[51]
Your house is God's house unless you associate yourself with devil.

Your "salvation"[52] is God's salvation, is God's joy, unless you reject his gospel and his teaching.

---

[51] Mt 22:37–39 NJB.
[52] Ps 62:2–3 NABRE.

BORN AGAIN

"Born again in the Spirit of God, not in the flesh."[53]
Born again when your heart is open to the kingdom of God and God's children.
Born again when you see God in every aspect of your life.
Born again when you, "love God, your neighbors and yourself."[54]

Born again when God helps you to achieve your goals and gives you wings to fly.
Born again when your heart and mind rest in God.
Born again when you see God in yourself, others, and everything that God created.
Born again when you are doing God's work, and you are blessed by Holy Trinity.

---

[53] Jn 3:1–10 NABRE.
[54] Mk 12:30–31 NABRE.

WINGS OF GOD

Wings of God, flying so high.
Wings of peace, safety is ours.
Wings of love, flow in our hearts.
Wings of hope, our lives rest in you.

Wings of forgiveness, erase our challenging memories if we truly repent and have deep contrition for our sins.
Wings of sincerity, purity, and security, we trust in our love.
Wings of "salvation,"[55] bless and save us all and bring us to eternal life.

---

[55] Ps 62:2–3 NABRE.

ANGELS OF GOD

Winged messengers of God bring us, "the Good News to lend strength to our bones."[56]
Angels of God, our safety is under your protection.
Winged messengers of God, help us travel with ease.

Winged messengers of God, help make our paths straight.
Angels of God, help clear the any obstacles that are in way.
Winged messengers, bring us God's love and Spirit.

---

[56] Prv 15:30 NJB.

CALL GOD

When the devil is at your doorstep, call God to rescue you.
When sins are your everyday activities, call God to rescue you.
"When the deceitful angels make you stand on the parapet of the temple,"[57] call God to rescue you.

When everything is not going your way or in the right direction, call God to rescue you.
When you seem to have faith but lack of will, call God to rescue you.
When you do things that are opposite to God's teachings, call God to rescue you.

When stress is sinking into your body, call God to rescue you.
When your loved one is suffering, call God to rescue them.
When you seem to lose hope, call God to rescue you.

---

[57] Mt 4:5 NABRE.

LOVE IS PURE

Love is what God brings to his children on a daily basis.
Love helps embrace diversity and reject barriers and adversities.
Love is the panacea for all the madness in the world.

Love helps rescind obstacles and open doors for many.

Love is a heart that is pure and clean with a million smiles.
Love helps bring joy to our hearts and revitalizes our spirits.
Love is the life that I live, the air that I breathe, the bread that I receive, and the wine that I drink.

Love is God's perfection in action, which flows in our spirits.

RESURRECTION

Resurrection of a man who had died long ago.
Resurrection of a man who left all sins behind.
Resurrection of man who follows the truth of the living God.

Resurrection of a man who sees God as his Father and carries God's image wherever he goes.
Resurrection of a man who stays out of darkness and stays in proximity to God's light.
Resurrection of a man who lives in the Spirit of God and does everything according to God's plan.

GOD IS SMILING

When the world is at peace, God is smiling.
When you love your relatives, your brothers, and sisters, God is smiling.
When your spirit is pure and clean in the eyes of God, God is smiling

When you forgive others for their mistakes, God is smiling.
When you embrace God's love and virtues, God is smiling.
When you love those who hurt you, God is smiling.

When your voice is inspiring through God's message, God is smiling.

YOUR DREAM

Your dream can disappear if you are not on the right track and not following God's teachings.

Your sin can multiply in astronomical numbers if you don't follow the truth.
Your love can diminish at any time if you don't keep it burning.
God's Spirit is not in your soul if you can't forgive others.

God's Spirit can extinguish from your soul if you don't follow his law.

Come to your Father; follow his Law and precepts.
Let God be the inspiration and the vehicle of your dream.
Embrace God's love and his people; always stay in his Spirit, and you will never falter.

SAVE A POOR SOUL

Lord, come back to a soul that is in desperate need of your assistance. God, come back and rescue a child whose sins are taking over his soul. Lord, embrace a child who is in desperate need of your love and your guidance.

Lord, rescue a child who has nothing good in him. God, save a poor soul who is on the brink of crashing. Lord, bring back to life a soul who lives in the dungeon and can't seem to see your light.

HIGHER ABOVE

Heaven is above all that exists.
Reign in our lives to save our world.
Human creation is the greatest of all that God has given us.
Higher above is the Ruler of all.
Father of love, rain in our dry desert to quench our thirst.
House of sunlight, shine in our lives.
Maker of all, rest in our hearts, and strengthen our weaknesses.
Creator of love, live in our lives to save our souls.

GOD'S WINGS

With God's wings, you can fly a million miles high; even on rainy days, everything that is obscure becomes clear.

With God's might, power, and wisdom, every complex issue becomes easy to rectify.

With God's strength, there is nothing that can stop your plans or your progress.

With God's wings, heaven is your limit, and its gates are wide open in the eyes of the faithful ones.

With God's wings, our hearts are open to all, even those who want to annihilate us.

SAILING THROUGH

Sailing through the ocean, but I don't know where it will lead me.
If I have real faith and love for God, He will spare me and steer me to the right place ashore.

Navigating through life, let God be my guide so that I can see the path, which will lead me back to Him.

Sailing with no knowledge of where I am heading.
If I can follow God's law and His guidance, my ship will steer in the right direction, and my path will be smooth.
Let the wind of God bless me and lead me to His kingdom.

IT'S TIME

Eating at God's table but working for the devil.
Attending church but disregarding the teachings of the gospel.
Pretending to love God, but you do not follow his law and precepts.
Pretending to be spiritual and God's disciple but empty of his Spirit.
It's time for you to stop pretending and stop doing the devil's work. It is time for you to carry God's love inside your heart.
It is time for you to embrace and love all God's children with no exception.
It is time for you to see the big picture, to start preparing yourself to be with God in the next life and for eternity.

WORLDLY THINGS ARE TRANSIENT

There is no paradise on earth unless you are in God's arms.

All the worldly things that you see on earth are transitory. The only three things that are not fleeting are the grace, the love, and the Spirit of God.

All the earthly things that you see are transient.

All the beautiful houses, the fast cars, all the superfluous money, and even your flesh will all be left behind.

The only thing that will last is when the Spirit of God enters your body and turns your soul into greatness for eternity.

REAL BEAUTY

Your beauty can be real inside and out if you can follow the law that your Father has created for you to follow; otherwise, you will have two faces if you are not following God.

When you think that some people with different ethnicities, backgrounds, ages, genders, classes are better than others, and you have no respect for the lives of others, you are cornering yourself to stay within the devil's framework.

When you do not follow any of God's commandments and disrespect the church, God's servants, and have no love for the bishops, priests, clergies, and deacons, God is not within you.

What a beautiful way to nourish your soul with the divine law that has been given freely to you by God.

What an awesome way to look beautifully inside and out when you follow God's law, teachings, and precepts, and you prepare yourself for the big prize.

You can certainly look more beautiful inside and out when you walk harmoniously with others in the Spirit and presence of God for the embellishment of God's kingdom.

YOU NEVER LET ME DOWN

Lord, you never let your children down when they are in distress; you won't let me down.
You are always there for me whenever I call upon your name.
Guide me, lead me, and rescue me because my ship is sinking faster than the blink of an eye. You are the only one who can save me.

You are the only God who is real, pure, mighty; you can spare me from this misery.

You are the only God who shows me true love whenever I am in shambles, in despair.
You are the true God that can resuscitate my soul, and all I have to do is to trust in your name. All I have to do is to trust in your miracles, your works, your love, and your guidance, and you will be there for me to quell my suffering.

A WORLD WITH NO MERCY

How can a world be so cruel and disregard everything that God has created?

When will they put priority in your Word and your works? What can we do to help show them your light?

When will the world live in peace and be a safe ground for your children?

How can we help rescind this madness that is destroying our children?

What are the positive steps that we can help them take to ameliorate the misery of God's children on earth?

What will it take to make that imperative step and to gain ground in our progress of helping to save the world?

How can we work as a unifying whole to make the world a better place for our children, God's children?

We just have to call upon God to give us strength, courage, and the ability to see what is right and wrong. We need to proclaim clearly the good news to our fellow citizens so that progress can be made.

COME IN, JOIN THE FEAST

"Lift up your heart,"[58] to "receive the gift of God."[59]
Open up your mind to see the wonders of God's kingdom.
Make your way to the church to be a part of the feast that is about
to begin.
Leave everything impure and unclean behind, and come to your
Father's house for this great celebration.

Come join the feast that is given to us by God and to receive the grace
that is pouring out to us from heaven.
Show your talent, your intellect, your wisdom from your voices to
your musical skills.
"Sing beautiful songs to the Lord,"[60] fill, "your hearts, minds, and souls
with happiness."[61]
Praise your Father endlessly, and let heaven see how wonderful its
servants and children are.

---

[58] Lam 3:41 NABRE.
[59] First Pt 4:10 NABRE.
[60] Ps 96:1–3 NABRE.
[61] Lk 10:27 NJB.

THANK GOD

How can you be so ungrateful to your Maker?
Why are you not obeying the Ten Commandments and thanking God for all that he has done for you?
Why do you have an ephemeral memory when it comes to giving accolades to God and praises to the One who loves you?

Why don't you thank God for, "his marvelous deeds,"[62] and use God's blessings to promulgate his Gospel?
Thank God for his love for you, give God praise for his grace, his blessings, and let your voice echo back the love that has been shown to you by your Father, your Maker, your God each and every day.

Why don't you thank God when you see the wonder of his work on earth? You questioned God instead of thanking Him.
How is it that you don't thank God when he does great things for you? But you have the audacity to ask the question of how did these things happened.

Can there be an explanation of how you can receive the grace of God and never thank God for the overflowing love and blessings that he pours out for you?

---

[62] Ps 3 NABRE.

LOVE

Love is kind, pure, clean, attractive, and never fading. It is always there for us: It is our minds, bodies, and souls that reject love sometimes when not in conformity with God's law.

Love does not discriminate when we all take the responsibility to follow the principles that have been put in place for us.

God's love is like water, elements of hydrogen and oxygen in a divine way that cannot be separated.

We can make positive impact and touch lives if we can spread God's love around the world.

Life without love is like a body with no soul, a human being without heart and lungs.

OPEN YOUR EYES!

You see the injustice, and you are not speaking out against it; you give us that tacit approach like you were never there.
You even closed your eyes when it was time to speak out against erroneous teachings and ignominious actions.
Please tell me why you are standing like a mule when you can help to "set others free"[63] and help abrogate those dubious claims.

Can you explain why you are letting them crucify those who don't have a voice and cannot speak for themselves?
Can you tell us why you are not letting the truth come out, giving everyone a piece of mind?

Why not live with the truth instead of burying yourself in lies?
Can you explain why you are not staying with God's intentions and actions and following what is beneficial to the world and God's children?
Why do you not see the light of God that is near to you, that can save so many lives, and set you free for eternity?

---

[63] Jn 8:32 NABRE.

GREAT HEART

A firm heart can be led by God; and its beats can bring rhythms of love and smiles to the world.

A good heart can bring your soul to the acme of love and good intentions.

A firm heart can make you see with clear eyes and win against all odds where the impossible can become the possible.

A great heart can help change and save the world.

A pure heart can see nothing but heaven as his or her future home.

STAY FIRM

Keep your eyes open wide, and stay vigilant because the devil can try to distract you and trick you to follow his lies.

Stay firm on your ground, and don't be malleable to the false prophets who are trying to "lead you astray."[64]

Ask God to help you resist the devil, to be able to distinguish and differentiate between good and evil.

Always ask God to help you to keep your focus on God at all times so that you don't get into the trickery game with the devil.

Ask God to keep you under his protection and to stay in your heart and spirit always. When you do this, nothing can trick you or make you do anything that would destroy your soul.

---

[64] First Jn 2:26 NJB.

WHY NOT SEE THE BIG PICTURE

Why allow the master of all deceits to obfuscate the truth and be risible to the good news?

Why let insanity take over your logical sense and allow the devil to manipulate the truth and lead you to the wrong path?

Why can't you see your true God right in front of you instead of following the devil?

Why can't you abandon the devil's works and take God as your true God?

When will you come to grip and embrace God, who can only save you?

YOUR WORDS

Lord Jesus, your truth is our guidance, and your words are our lives when we follow them.

Your words open doors, hearts, and minds and bring our world to another level.

Your truth helps us open our hearts to others, and your eyes help us to be good stewards.

Your words help bring clarity to all things that are obscure and nebulous.

Your words never end; they live in those who have great intentions, and they are here to stay to "set your people free."[65]

Our lives would be obsolete without your caring, your grace, your love, and your presence around us.

---

[65] Jn 8:32 NJB.

LIVING DREAM

Living the real dream on earth when I can love my brothers and sisters.
Living the real dream on earth when I can praise God with all my heart.
Living the real life on earth when vanities are not priorities in my life.

Living the true dream on earth when I can go to church and eat at my Lord's table.
Living the real life on earth when I see every person as a child of God.
Living a true dream life when God is my only answer, and my heart belongs to God.

TRYING TO UNDERSTAND

I don't understand how one can associate himself or herself with the devil who sins, lies, and destroys souls on a quotidian basis.

I am still trying to understand God's kingdom better so that I can proclaim it in a better way to my brothers and sisters.

I came from a long way, Lord. I came to understand that you, no other god, can possess the love that you have for your children. "There is no other God like you Lord."[66]

If I cannot see your goodness among the living, then I am no longer alive, and I am still living in sin.

Your love for us is sufficient for me to believe that you are the true, real, and eternal living God. If I don't have the eyes to see that Lord, give me the intellect, the vision, and the ability to understand your way better.

---

[66] First Kings 8:23 NJB.

TREE OF LIFE AND LOVE

Tree of life, feed all your children with all the good fruits.
Tree of love, soften the hearts of those who have nothing to offer.
Tree of life, let your children see the radiance and the light of your love.

Tree of all life and love, open the hearts of your children so that they can live by your words.

Tree of life, give your children the intellect with great common sense to survive in this world.
Tree of love, the living, and the dead, you are always there for all to see.
Tree of life, help us to see the greatness of a living God.

GOD OF ALL

God of all, your love never ends, even when we falter.

God of hosts, you never stop doing good deeds and never stop giving to your children, even when we stop thanking you for what you have done for us.

Gracious living God, your grace never stops pouring on us, even when we don't understand the nature of your kingdom.

"Everlasting God,"[67] your love is always fresh and new.

Some days I wake up and ask myself, "How can you love me so much and always keep me by your side?" I have absolutely nothing good in me, Lord.

Lord, how can I give the love back to you the same way that you love me and be with you forever?

How can I worship you all day long, and how can your kingdom become my kingdom?

Lord of all, how can my body become your body and my blood become your blood, my love become your love, my spirit become your Spirit, and I become part of you?

---

[67] Is 40:28 NJB.

RADIANCE OF GOODNESS

Radiance of life, live in our world and transform us to goodness.
Thunder of love, come to our world, flow in our lives, and make our hearts pure.
Rain of life and love, pour in our hearts and minds, and transform us to everything that is good and beneficial to our lives.

Lightning of love, strike our hearts with love and kindness, and help us to love one another.
Rainbow of love, show us your true colors so that we can live by the examples of your law.
Snow of life and love, fall in our day, bring purity and liberty into our world.

CANNOT LIVE WITHOUT GOD

How long will it take for you to come to grips that you cannot live without God?

If you think that you can, then you are not among the living on earth.

When will you get a full grasp of how God's law works to your benefit?

When will you see the plan that God has set for you so that you may see Him again?

If you are not there, then God is not in you, and your soul and mind are saturated with nonsense.

When will you become adept with God's law and principles?

How long will it take for you to stop living in madness and embrace the love that your Father has given to you at no cost?

When will the kingdom of God be in, "your heart, mind, and soul"[68] and love be your everyday meal?

---

[68] Lk 10:27 NJB.

REST IN YOUR ARMS

When I can't seem to find the light at the end of the tunnel, let me rest in your arms.

When I can't seem to do anything right, let me rest in your arms.
When my world is at loss, let me rest in your arms.
When the devil is at my doorstep, let me rest in your arms.

When sadness and sorrow take over my normal activities, let me rest in your arms.

When my life is in shambles, and I don't know where to go, let me rest in your arms.
When the world's temper is flared, and I don't know where to hide, let me rest in your arms.
When my world is on the verge of crashing, let me rest in your arms.

When I feel like I am hopeless and helpless, let me rest in your arms.

LIVE IN THE PRESENCE OF CHRIST

You live in Christ, and Christ lives in you when you follow that natural law.

You live in Christ when you start loving your brothers and sisters and focus on Him like a laser and never leave his side.

You live in Christ when you let your spirit be his Spirit, let his love stay in your heart, and let his intentions take over your soul.

You live in Christ, and Christ lives in you when you stay with his Spirit and do what is acceptable in his eyes.

You live in Christ when you put in all the hard work, and you follow his law.

You live in Christ when you love him and his people. If you can follow these principles, there will be no other place for you to live but heaven.

BLESS AND SAVE ME

Bless me now while I am alive.

Save me now while you are mine, and I am yours.

Bless me now while I am at your house and see no other gods but you.

Save me now while my mind is focused on you and only you.

Bless me now while I am in you, and let heaven be my ultimate prize.

Save and bless me now while I see you unequivocally as my ultimate Savior and the only route to heaven.

STOP WORRYING ABOUT PAYBACK

You think that you are giving everything that you have and getting nothing in return.

You think you are showing all the love that you can to others and getting nothing in return in this earthly world.

You think you are helping everybody finish their tasks and fulfilling their dreams, but no one is helping you.

"Will you lay down your life for your brothers and sister,"[69] when you think that you get nothing in return?

Will you do everything that you think is possible to help your fellow citizens, even when you don't think that you get something in return? Can you do all you can and stop worrying about what you are getting in return?

Are you able to see the big picture that is in front of you and be able to see that God will give you wings to fly when you do good works?

If you can do good and never worry about the payback, your good works will not go in vain, and you will be like a star shining in heaven.

---

[69] Jn 15:13 NJB

COMPLAINING

The work has not even begun, and you are already complaining.
You just took one step toward the climbing mountain, and you are already complaining about fatigue and the strenuous work you are doing.
What will you do when you take a few more steps forward?

You are not even laying down the bricks, and you are already complaining of too much work.
Do you think that you will get a pass to go to heaven for doing absolutely nothing on earth to strengthen God's kingdom?
What will you do when you get the full responsibility from God to help guide and lead his people?

What will you do when God calls you to climb the mountain more than three times?
Will you see the vision and the plan that your Father has for you to help make the world better? If you do, then you are on the path that will lead you to God.

GOD WILL

God will guide and lead you the same way that you guide and lead his people.

If you chose the devil's path, you will find that is not God's choice for you. That is your own choice because God does not want to tie your hands and said, "Follow me." It is God, "who wills everyone to be saved and come to the knowledge of the truth."[70]

It is up to you to make the right decision. It's up to you to make the choice that will lead to God.

God will love you and care for you the same way that he has shown love to his people. Even if God is not in your soul and you have no love for his people, he still loves you.

God will spare you the same way that you spare his people and help save life on earth. Take note! All the good works that you do will help lead you to your heavenly Father.

[70] Tm 2:4 NABRE.

LET GOD BE YOUR VEHICLE

Let God be your leader, and you be the facilitator of his work.

Let God be the provider, and you be the receiver.

Let God be your guidance and your vehicle so that you can be led in the right direction.

Let God be your light so that you can help get others out of darkness.

Let God be your grace so that you can start loving others like he does.

Let God be your source of food so that you can help feed others with all the goodness.

Let God be a positive influence in your life so that you help build others up.

Let God spare your life so that you can help open the eyes of others and help save their lives.

YOUR CHILDREN NEED HELP

The children are dying, but there is not enough help to reach them, and there are just a few people who are willing to plead for their cause. The children are starving, but there is not enough food to give them to share.

Their lives are being taken each and every day, but we disregard our duty of serving the children of God.

Lord, will you intervene to save your children because you are the only one who can put a stop to this madness. You are the only one who can bring peace to the world. You are the only one who can soften their hearts and minds and help your children to live in tranquility. Lord, you are the only one who can save the world and protect our children.

KINGDOM OF GOD

"Lord, You have told us that your Kingdom does not belong to this world."[71]
Could it be right above us, and we just don't have the capacity and the ability to see it?
Can all the good deeds that we have done on earth lead us back to you?

Your kingdom is higher above; how can we reach it?
Will it take one step of your ladder to reach heaven if we follow your way day and night?
Could your kingdom be right between our eyes, and we don't see it?

Can we take a pause for a minute and ask ourselves, "Why are we asking all of these questions?" The kingdom of God is right in front of us. We have to live it in order to see it. We have to be on the same page as God to be able to see his kingdom.

---

[71] Jn 18:36 NABRE.

LIVING GOD

Mighty God in the sky, keep us alive and new in this fleeting world.
Living God and heavenly King, bring to us your blessings with a smile.
Eternal God in the high place, live in our hearts with infinite time.

High Priest with abundant love, let your grace flow like pouring rain
on your children.
True divine, live in our time, and bring us the peace that we deserve.
"Loving God, rest in our heart, mind, and spirit."[72] Bring us the love
and peace that the earth cannot give.

---

[72] Lk 10:27 NJB.

PEACE FROM ABOVE

Peace on earth, makes heaven smile.
Doing philanthropic work around the globe must be the agape love that is in your heart.
Living in peace, tranquility is at its peak.
Bringing us love, God's law is in action.
Keep on smiling, heaven is on your side.
You have the metanoia in your, "heart, mind and soul,"[73] that must be the Spirit of God within.
God's Grace is pouring around you; this is just the beginning.

---

[73] Lk 10:27 NJB.

CHANGE IS HERE!

When the Spirit of God comes near your tent, you will be a new man. When God's presence dwells in your soul, you will see the world though a different lens.

When the heavenly Spirit touches your heart, you will spread God's love all over earth.

When God's love reigns in your heart and spirit and soul, it will wash clean every single cell of your body to make it pure.

When God's message flows into your brain, your world will change forever.

When heavenly grace plunges into your soul, then you will begin to change the life of many with God's help.

STAY OPEN

Never question the power of God.
Let your faith in God be a reflection of your thinking.
Never take for granted your place at God's table.

Never procrastinate when it comes to doing what is good for the kingdom of God.
Let your mind be the receptor of the great knowledge from God.
Never let fatigue take of your spiritual growth or your learning curve.

Always be attentive and adroit when it comes to facilitating God's will. Always be open to the divine grace that God is giving you.

FANTASY WORLD

Stop living for others when you can be in God's Spirit instead.

Stop trying to impress sinners, and give your heart to God.

Let the Spirit of God take your soul to another level.

Stop trying to impress a world that is fraught with deceits and that cannot save you.

Stop living in the past, and let God's missions be at the center of your life.

Let God be the one that you want to impress and follow his true and divine law.

Stop living in sin, and let God rescue your soul from, "the unclean spirits, depraved hearts and corrupt minds."[74]

Let God be your living bread and wine every single day!

---

[74] First Tm 6:3-5 NABRE.

HELP!

Help deliver the message and the blessing that God has sent for his people.

Help those who are lost find paradise.

Do your best to deliver the good news to this transitory world.

Make great efforts to unify those who are divided, and help bring peace to their world.

Help establish God's law and principles; where there is confusion, help restore God's Spirit among the unfaithful.

Help those enjoy the life that God wants for all of his children.

Help God's children smile again for heaven's sake, and make your Father proud.

CRYING OUT TO GOD

Father, I am crying out to you.

Why am I struggling so much to take care of my everyday responsibilities?

Why is the road so steep and strenuous to climb?

Sometimes I feel like my heart is not beating at a regular pace, and my head has too many things to dissect and intercept.

Sometimes I wonder, *Why can't I have enough to take care of this beautiful family that I have?*

Why can't everything be facile for my mind, brain, and my eyes to accept my everyday life?

Why can't I see the sunrise and sunset in a twelve-hour day?

Why can't heaven hear me cry and rescind my struggles?

I have to be patient and stand still because God knows what my necessities are. He is a God of love, mercy, and hope. He will answer me when I, "knock on his door," and rescue me when I am on the brink of sinking.

PEACE

Peace can open the airways for us to breath.

Great understanding can open the gate of love and bring God's children together.

Love can be a treasure that we can cherish in our hearts and help them to beat at normal pace

Peace can make the world a tranquil environment for all to live and to enjoy the life and blessings that God has in store for us.

Peace, sincerity, understanding, love, and kindness can lead us to our Father with ease when we prophesize, "help magnify the word of God,"[75] and help it to reach its destination.

---

[75] Ps 34:2–3 NABRE.

STOP DOING THE DEVIL'S WORK

Stop doing the devil's work; come to God's senses, Spirit, and start doing things right.

Stop vitiating those who don't have guidance and don't know where to go.

Stop being too complacent; get up, and help pass the message to those who are in dire need to hear the good news.

Stop being fraudulent, and help the children in our society to grasp the gospel.

Stop the tirade against others and, "come to the knowledge of the Truth."[76]

Stop being so distant from others; come close, and help do the right thing.

Stop running around with your specious arguments and stay with the truth.

Stop being so submissive to the devil, and open your hearts to God.

---

[76] Second Tm 3:7.

EVER LIVING GOD

Omnipotent God, open the gates of heaven, and let us see your greatness.
Heavenly God, let your divine grace flow in our lives to bring us joy and happiness.
Omnipotent God, open the gates of heaven to all who believe, and let them see your sanctuary.

Ever present God, let your Spirit fly high to bring good news to your children.
Ever living God, open the hearts of those who do not know you yet, and help them come to the conclusion that your way is the only route to your heavenly kingdom.

INSANITY IS NOT PART
OF GOD'S MISSION

Obscurity is not God's plan; it's the devil's.

Confusion is not in God's nature; it's the devil's.

Division is nowhere near God's Spirit; it's the devil's.

Obfuscation is not part of God's mission; it's the devil's.

False conspiracy is not God's way but the devil's.

Love, care, kindness, and peace are what is permissible in the Lord's household.

All the confusion, division, hatred, and myopic minds on earth are not God's way; they're the devil's!

Now is the time for you to start loving God, respect his house, and embrace his children.

WHY?

Why are you so impetuous to take actions when something is in your way?

Remember what Jesus said, "offer no resistance to one who is evil. When someone strikes you on [your] right cheek, turn the other one to him as well."[77]

Why are you so quarrelsome when you can live in peace and harmony with your brothers and sisters?

Why are you living in the past when you can move on, forget, and forgive, and look to a bright future ahead?

Why are you always part of the transgressions when you can be a mediator and be part of the peace process?

Why are you living in insanity when you can give your whole heart to God?

---

[77] Mt 5:39 NABRE.

LOVE

Love is the catalyst of the Spirit of God.
Love is what transforms a world to peacefulness and tranquility.
Love is what makes the world move forward on positive notes.

Love is when, "God's Spirit is magnified,"[78] and has exemplified goodness in you.
Love is the nature of a great and an awesome God in action.
Love is when God's grace kisses your heart, embracing your mind and spirit for the better of our world.

---

[78] Ps 34:2–4 NABRE.

RATHER BE WITH GOD

When you debunk false claims, they accuse you of judging. I would rather stay with the truth.

I would rather speak the truth than be caught lying to God's people.

I would rather put my trust in a true living God than trust other gods who cannot save.

I would rather die with the truth, than live in lies.

I would rather live in God than be associated with the devil.

I would rather suffer a great deal than disrespect God's table.

I would rather have nothing than to have everything and not be able to help the poor, who are in dire need.

HEAVENLY LOVE

O heavenly love, live in my soul forever blessed.

O great divine, speak to me now, and let every part of my, "heart, mind, and soul,"[79] listen to the sound of your blessed voice.

O heavenly love, bring to life the vision of your love, and place in my heart the Spirit of your kingdom.

O great divine, bring clarity, sincerity, and purity to my world.

O heavenly love, let your Spirit be voice, my vision, knowledge, and my prolific way of thinking.

O heavenly love, let your Spirit take me and guide me to the path that will lead me to you.

---

[79] Lk 10:27 NJB.

HEAVEN'S CALL

When my mother comes to give me the heads-up three months ahead of my time, heaven is calling.
When others mourn and grieve for me, heaven is calling.
When you see me in a box, and I can no longer speak and walk, heaven is calling.

When you see me at my brother's church on earth for the last time, heaven is calling.
When God's angels are waiting for me at the gate, heaven is wide open to welcome its newest member.
When my brother, my Father, and the Holy Spirit smile at me with great accolades, heaven is reached.

GIVE ME STRENGTH

Lord, give me the wings of an eagle to fly high.
Give me the eyes of an eagle to see in daylight.
Bring me the joy that no one else can bring but you.
Give me the eyes of an owl to see in the dark.
Infuse in me a reflex faster than the speed of light.
Give me the strength of a dung beetle, an eagle, an African bush elephant, and a blue whale to fight adversity, to embrace love and diversity for your people.
Make me the strongest human being on earth to fight for your people's rights and help bring your message to your people.

BETTER VISION IN GOD

You cannot see anything beyond God unless you are a part of God's plan.

You won't be able to catch the unseen unless you are part of the mystical body.

"You cannot see the kingdom of God unless you open your heart to God and his children."[80]

You cannot see the kingdom of God unless you can see the vision that God has in store for you.

You won't be able to have a divine mind if you are not in the same line with God's imaginary line.

You cannot speak in tongues, have scripture knowledge, and spread the good news unless the Spirit of God is in you.

You cannot see beyond the earth unless you are one of the chosen ones.

You can see everything when God's Spirit is in, "your mind, body, and soul,"[81] and you become part of the ever living God.

---

[80] Jn 3:3 NJB.
[81] Mt 22:37 NABRE

HELP YOUR CHILDREN, LORD

Lord, help change a world that has no respect for your law or your children.

Help change those with myopic views and desiccated minds.

Help those who are eager to take the journey that will lead them back to you.

Give the children the tools they need in order to succeed in this life.

Help your children to see the trace of your life, and help them to follow it until the end.

Help sharpen your servants' minds in order to evangelize and spread the good news in a better and effervescent way.

Help soften those with stoic hearts, and help change the minds of those with bad intentions and visions that are contrary to your law.

KEEP YOUR MIND UP

Listen to the good news! Don't let the devil distract you from your plan and rain on your parade.
Live your life in an enjoyable and ebullient way; make the best of it. Always try to do the right thing; don't let the devil infiltrate you with all sorts of madness.

Stay adroit; keep your mind sharp. Always be ready to learn new things that will be beneficial to you, your children, your fellow citizens, and the kingdom of God.

Stay focused on what is important in your life; let your body take the full assimilation of its core.
Respect others, and do all the things that you think will lead you to God.
Put your mind in God's mission, and you will live in the reality of his law and his kingdom.

THE SPIRIT OF GOD KEEPS ME ALIVE

My world is at peace when I can sing and praise the Lord at church.

My heart is filled with joy when I am at my brother's house.

My life is above ground, and I am no longer buried when I can see God every single day amongst the living.

My mind is at rest because the Spirit of the living is in me, and God is the testimony of my life.

My spirit is no longer mine when I am in God and God is in me.

My boat is always floating when I have the Spirit of God in me, with great vision to accomplish great missions.

NEVER GIVE UP!

Never give up on God or yourself when you know that God is your ticket to heaven.

Never give up on your good deeds when you know that they will help you reach heaven.

Always be in alliance with God and his Spirit; you will never fall into darkness or, "go astray."[82]

Never take the Word of God for granted; always follow the good news and the truth, which is the ultimate route to God.

Always show love to people around you so that they can see God in you and your intentions.

---

[82] Is 53:6 NJB.

SEARCHING

Searching for the living among the dead.
Looking for the faithful in a world full of sin.
Searching for heaven in this earthly world.

Searching for water when the well runs dry.
Looking for the truth in a world full of lies and corruption.
Searching for answers, while others are trying to hide the truth.

Searching for life in the city of death.
Searching for my Creator to give me all the blessings that I need.
I won't stop looking until I find Him.

GIVE ME

Lord of all, give me the love and the life that the world cannot provide me.

Bring me the blessings and the knowledge that only I can receive and no one else can give but you.

Rest in my soul eternally.

Give me the brain of an intellect, and make my mind as sharp as a razor blade.

I see and live in the presence of a true living God, who has never stopped loving.

My spirit lives in peace when God is in me, and my heart beats with joy when God's love flows in my soul.

STAY WITH GOD

Bow down to a true living God.

"Trust wholeheartedly in Yahweh, put no faith in your own perception; acknowledge Him in every course you take, and He will see that your path is smooth."[83]

Stay in God's boundaries, and you'll be under his loving care and safety.

Pray to a God who never stops loving and is always present.

Keep your heart and mind in the true living and your will never falter.

Live with the truth, and you will never have to worry.

Learn how to love so that you'll never stop caring.

---

[83] Prv 3:5–6 NJB.

LIVE IN GOD

Live in the Spirit of a true living God.
Stay in my soul while your Spirit blesses my nest.
Bless your children on earth.
Live in my soul, and give me the life of a good steward in today's society.
"Let your people sing your song to you and praise you all day long,"[84] in order to elevate their faith.
Give life to those who don't have it yet and those waiting for their God to lead the way.
Live in my world, and change my whole life to become a servant of yours.

---

[84] Ps 96:1–3 NIV.

KEEP YOUR FOCUS

When your spirit is rested in the flesh, your soul is a mess.

If your mind is bonded to this world, you turn into dust.

When your intentions and actions belong to this world, you have an empty nest.

If vanity is your god, your mind will never rest.

When you don't follow God's principles, and your heart belongs to this world, your mind will never rest.

If God is not in your soul, you have no love in you; your future is at risk, and it needs newness.

THE ONLY TRUE GOD

Our God is real! What other God would be bonded with love forever? Can you think of any other god who never waivers and always forgives his children?

The presence of God around makes me tacit sometimes; I cannot think of any word that can describe the greatness of God.

What other gods would allow us to get up just as many times as we fall and never stop loving us?

What kind of God would sacrifice his only Son so that the gates of heaven may be open to all of those who have trust in him?

ONLY SAY GOOD THINGS

Help spread the love of God around the globe.

Stay away from anything that would be detrimental to your friends and others.

Don't let Satan obviate your good intentions or actions from reaching your brothers and sisters.

Keep away from any incendiary words; always say good things about others, and keep the Spirit of God in you.

Refrain yourself from nonsense, myopic views; help your fellow citizens to see the light of God. Help your friends and others see the reality of the living God, who is right here, right now, with us.

STAY THE COURSE

When your spirit is in God, love is in your heart. There is no need to worry about anything because you are in God's hand.

There is no better place that you can be than to be in the hand of the Almighty.

There are no other gods who can protect you, love you, and care for you like the true living God.

Keep up the good work, be conducive in every mission and plan that you undertake in order to facilitate God's work.

Stay true to God's law, and then stay focused on the tasks that will help open the gates of heaven for you.

WHY FOLLOW STRANGE GODS?

Why follow the devil?

Why follow some fallible gods that can lead you to nowhere but the bottom?

Why do the devil's work, which can only destroy your soul and lead you to a dead end?

Why behave in a way that is contrary to your Creator's law and teachings?

Tell me, why is your mind so focused on things that have no value and no future according to God's law?

Why not focus on the things that are imperative and helpful to yours and others' lives?

Open your eyes, keep your mind straight, and stay focused on a God that can only save—if you follow the truth.

LOSS OF LOVED ONES

Lord, you always tell me to stop mourning for the dead for years because it's not good for my health.

I have this pain inside me that never goes away, especially when I think of my loves that I've spent time with, who were always close to me. My excruciating pain is burning inside me when I think of the loss of my loved ones.

Help me to be at ease, help my pain to go away, help my heart to start beating at a normal pace, help me to stop worrying about the past and to stay focus on you.

Help me to rescind the struggles that I have, and pray for my loved ones who've left this world to live with your words, your prayers, and your Spirit so that I can go on and live the life that you blessed me with.

WHY?

Why love a fruit that is forbidden in the eyes of God?
Why imitate the sin or follow the direction of the devil when your heart can rest in God?
Why be an adventurer when you can be an evangelizer?

Why stare at a diamond that does fit not your finger?
Why live in a fantasy world when you can stay clean and pure and live with God for eternity?

Why fall into sin when you can fall in the arms of God?
Why let the devil win a battle that is for you to win?
Why destroy your soul when you can live in the Spirit of God?

GOD FORGIVES!

God never leaves you. You are the one who steps away from Him.
God always loves you. You are the one who stops loving God, yourself, your friends, and your neighbors.
God always cares for you. You are the one who stops caring for God's law, plans, missions, and your brothers and sisters.
God always welcome you back when you fall into sin, but you must truly repent; you are the one who stops forgiving others for their mistakes.
You have free will, but I encourage you to come to God and embrace God's efforts to meet you halfway so that God can lead you to His kingdom.

REST YOUR SOUL IN GOD

Leave everything behind to embrace a true living God.

Don't do anything that will separate you from your Father.

Come to your senses, and allow God to help you make the right decisions.

Live a live that is acceptable to God and to your brothers and sisters.

Help pave the road and your path; make them smooth and easy so that they can lead you to your Father.

Bear in your soul the Spirit of your Creator.

Live a life that is pure, and rest in God; he will bless you with a cornucopia of grace.

Prepare your bed for the future in order to have a chance to live with God in his sanctuary.

GOD AND LOVE

God is life
Where there is no love, there is no God, there is no life, and love is obsolete.
God is goodness and love.
If love is not in your world, God does not exist inside your heart because God and love are cohesive and intertwine with each other. The two do not leave each other one step behind.
God's love never ends. It's always there, and it always brings light to our world.
God's love is here to stay forever and ever.

CITY OF PEACE

City of peace, where tranquility exists.

White buildings and skyscrapers are full of stars around them.

City of peace, where the grass is greener than green, angels and saints are everywhere.

City of peace, where love always exists, and hearts are always pure. There is nothing like it on earth. It's where God's love is peaked and where all the blessed ones rest.

City of peace, where spirits are alive and pure, and love is the norm for eternity.

ONLY GOD AND THOSE IN HIS SPIRIT TRULY FORGIVE

There is a phrase that states, "To err is human, to forgive is divine."
If you make mistakes in your life, take a good look at how the world reacts when you apologize and ask for forgiveness.

You ask the world for forgiveness, but you might get crucified after your apology.

Don't wait for a world that does not forgive to forgive you. It may never come your way from this world; move on with your life, and sin no more.

Those who associate with the devil do not believe in forgiveness, but those who are in the Spirit of God can truly forgive, even if they are affected by your actions.

GOD OF ABRAHAM

"God of Abraham,"[85] open the gates of heaven for all of your children to see.

"God of hosts,"[86] the road is strenuous, and we are failing; give us strength and help keep us on your path.

"God of Jacob," open the eyes and the hearts of a world that cannot see, hear, love, or listen.

"God with mighty power,"[87] let the world see your power and help your children to embrace your kingdom.

"God of Isaac," let your children see your abundant love and grace flowing upon them.

"God of the meek and humble,"[88] open the minds of all; help them to think right and make the right decisions so that they can better follow your law.

"God of all,"[89] bring your blessings upon this world and make it brand new.

---

[85] Acts 3:13 NJB.

[86] Dt 10:17 NJB.

[87] Eph 1:19–23 NJB.

[88] Mt 11:30; 2 Cor 10:1 NJB.

[89] Second Cor 1:3–5 NJB.

YOUR LOVE

Thirty-three years of misery and greatness.

Those who do not know your kingdom do not know your children either.

You opened the gates of heaven for a world that had no chance of reaching it.

You sacrificed your whole life to save a world that still does not understand the nature of a living God.

You make me think of a God who has no boundaries with his love, might, and grace.

Forgive me, my Lord, I misunderstood. I never thought that you would love me the way that you do.

Your love is like playing a violin on a rainy day, which embellishes its beauty even more.

IF YOU WOULDN'T EXIST
WITHOUT GOD

Look at the trees, the flowers, and the plants; they all have different shapes and colors, but they all contribute to the beauty of the earth. Look at the human race; we all have different tones of skin, hair, eye color, but we are all children of a living God, who has never stopped loving.
Look at the air, the breeze, and how the wind blows, and tell me that there is not a living God among us.

Look at all the things that God has created for us to see his grace, love, mighty power, and realize that your Creator is here among us. Can you pause a minute and just take a look at yourself, and tell me that you are not among the greatest of God's creations on earth? Look at your mindset, your visions, all the love and great spirits around you, and tell me that your Creator, your God, your Lord is here with you.

LAMENTATION

I cried out loud to God and asked Him for the world to be at peace. I prayed to the Holy Father to keep us in his tabernacle.

I think about the present and future for my children to be at peace. I ask God for mercy for those living in sin and who can't seem to find the light.

I am waiting for the world to change its course, but it might never come.

I pray for those who can't seem to get it right and need some guidance. I pray for rain to fall where there is a fire of destruction in our midst. I know that heaven will hear my cry, my misery, my tribulation, and trepidation and come to the rescue of those who are in desperate need.

HEAVEN IS NEAR

"Trumpets will sound loud and clear,"[90] but your faith will decide your destination.

Heaven is near; bring the most beautiful flower on earth to welcome your Lord for his second coming.

Heaven is here; sing all the great songs to welcome the Lord and his company.

Christ's face is in the sky, "but will not touch this sinful ground with his feet."[91] You will see his mother, too, after his face appears in the sky.

This will be a day of joy when our Savior comes to carry us to his Holy Place.

The earth will rejoice to see the Son of Man right between its eyes. All of God's children will gather to follow and enter heaven's gates.

[90] Rv 8:6 NJB.
[91] First Thes 4:17 NJB.

STAY WITH THE LORD

Never let hypocrisy and abnormality settle in your soul.

Never let hateful thinking be your vehicle or guidance.

Let the Lord be your navigator, your leader, and your Savior for eternity.

Never carry any animosity toward those who are at fault, but always pray to the Lord for them, rescue them from misery.

Never let selfishness and avarice take over your soul. Always do the right thing so you may live a life with no regrets.

Let the Lord help you see the light that will ultimately lead you to heaven.

Let Christ be in everything that you do so that you will have a chance to live with Him forever.

I AM AT PEACE AND EASE WITH YOU

Lord, my place is not here on earth but with you in heaven.

My dream will not be fulfilled until I see you.

My mind, heart, and soul will not be at peace until I clearly see heaven with my eyes.

I will not need wings to fly because my heavenly Lord will provide me with enough helium to stay afloat.

I will have a new name and rank within the company of the saints.

There is nothing that I will need, and my glass will be full.

My dreams, my hard work, my vision, and my thinking will be cohesive to yours eternally.

STAY WITH GOD

Lord, When I was at the age of three, you spared me from the lion's mouth.

Those who belong to the devil thought I was sold to the devil, and I was a dead child walking.

But what the evil minds didn't understand is that I am a child of God. One cannot take what belongs to God; like Jesus said, "pay to Caesar what belongs to Caesar—and God what belongs to God."[92]

I began to fully understand that the devil cannot take what belongs to Almighty God.

That is why I encourage you today to keep your focus on God. If you don't, you will become weak and vulnerable to those offering only evil.

Keep your eyes on your Creator. Stay prudent and vigilant, but do not be afraid of anything because when God is with you, you can fly on rainy days with your feathers.

When God is with you, you become impervious to those with malicious intent. Even if your flesh were to leave you, you will live with God forever.

---

[92] Mk 12:17 NJB; Mt 22:15–22 NJB; Lk 20:25 NJB.

A TRUE GOD

I see a true living God among us who erased my worries and comes to my rescue every time.

I see a God who never stops caring or loving his children, and a God who has every great intention.

I cannot think of any other God like our Creator. His overflow of love, his caring, his grace never leave us.

How can one not love his Creator, his Father, his Maker the way he or she should?

Father, I do not know how to thank you enough for all the great things that you have done for me.

When I think of you, Father, I think of a true living Father, a true living God, a true Creator whose love for his children never ends.

STAY ON TRACK

Be sure to stay on the right course, and keep your mind on God and God alone.
Stay close to what can be your future eternal joy and happiness.
Help make your path smooth, and follow the route that will ultimately lead you to God.
Keep your dream awake and alive; don't follow the devil, and you will be fine.

Do and say all the great things that will make your Father proud and help prepare a space for you in your "Father's house."[93]
Live in accordance with your Father's law, and you will be blessed.
Do good at all times and make your case to your Father in order to reach that beatific vision.

---

[93] Jn 14:2 NJB.

GOD IS ALWAYS HERE

Rain and snow come and go; so does our admiration for others.
Day and night come and go; so does our love and good intentions.
God's love does not leave us for one bit. He is a caring and loving
Father, who never stops loving his children.
Morning and evening separate themselves for twelve hours.

The only one who does not separate himself from his children and
from you is God.
He is the only God who does not alienate and abandon his children.
With him we can see the truth and the Spirit of a true living God
who is our Maker, our loving Father, and our God.

94

---

94 Rv 8:1–13 NJB.

SOURCES

Printed in the United States
by Baker & Taylor Publisher Services